How do you put sparkle in a blonde's eyes?
(See page 7)

What's a blonde's mating call?
(See page 10)

What do you call a blonde who's dyed her
hair brown?
(See page 13)

How do you get a blonde to marry you?
(See page 15)

What did the blonde write home from her vacation?
(See page 49)

How can you tell a blonde who's really conceited?
(See page 61)

Also by Blanche Knott
Published by St. Martin's Press

TRULY TASTELESS JOKES IV
TRULY TASTELESS JOKES V
TRULY TASTELESS JOKES VI
TRULY TASTELESS JOKES VII
TRULY TASTELESS JOKES VIII
TRULY TASTELESS JOKES IX
TRULY TASTELESS JOKES X
TRULY TASTELESS JOKES XI
TRULY TASTELESS ANATOMY JOKES
TRULY TASTELESS ANATOMY JOKES II
TRULY TASTELESS DOCTOR JOKES
TRULY TASTELESS LAWYER JOKES
TRULY TASTELESS MILITARY JOKES
TRULY TASTELESS KENNEDY JOKES
BLANCHE KNOTT'S BOOK OF TRULY TASTELESS
ETIQUETTE
THE WORST OF TRULY TASTELESS JOKES
(HARDCOVER)
THE TRULY TASTELESS JOKE-A-DATE BOOK

Blanche Knott's

Truly Tasteless

Blonde

Jokes

SMP

ST. MARTIN'S PAPERBACKS

TRULY TASTELESS BLONDE JOKES

Copyright © 1992 by Blanche Knott.

All rights reserved. No part of this book may be used or reproduced in any manner whatsoever without written permission except in the case of brief quotations embodied in critical articles or reviews. For information address St. Martin's Press, 175 Fifth Avenue, New York, N.Y. 10010.

ISBN: 0-312-92969-2

Printed in the United States of America

St. Martin's Paperbacks edition/May 1992

10 9 8 7 6 5 4 3 2 1

to Juliette

What does a blonde say after sex?
  "So, are all you guys on the same team?"

•

How does a blonde turn on the light after sex?
  Opens the car door.

•

Why does a blonde wear pantyhose?
  To keep her ankles warm.

A young pastor married a cute blonde who'd been around with lots of guys while he himself had little sexual experience. On their wedding night he stepped into the bathroom to put on his pajamas, and when he came out he was shocked to find his new wife lying nude on the bed. Alarmed, he blurted out, "I thought I would find you on your knees by the side of the bed."

"Nah," said the blonde, "that position always gives me the hiccups."

•

Why did the aging blonde have her tubes tied?
    So she wouldn't have any more grandchildren.

•

How many blondes does it take to change a light bulb?
    One—to hold the bulb and wait for the world to revolve around her.

The old farmer and his wife were sitting on their porch after celebrating their fiftieth wedding anniversary. At long last the wife, her golden hair long since turned to silver, broke the peaceful silence with a question. "Have you ever been unfaithful to me?"

"Once, dear, just once," quavered her husband. "And you?"

"Just a minute," she said and disappeared into the house, returning with a shoebox containing six kernels of corn and twenty thousand dollars in cash.

Her husband gaped at her. "What the hell does this mean?"

"Every time I'm unfaithful to you, I put a kernel of corn in the box," she explained.

"Well, what's the money for?"

His wife said, "Every time I get a bushel, I sell it."

•

How can you tell if a blonde has a blond boyfriend?

There're bruises around her navel.

•

If a blonde and a brunette jump out of a building, who lands first?

The brunette. The blonde has to stop and ask for directions.

•

"Now cheer up, Paul," soothed his buddy Bill over a couple of Budweisers. "You and Louise seem to be doing just fine. And it seems a little silly for you to be jealous of a German shepherd. After all, you work all day and you live out in the sticks. That dog's good company for Louise."

"Good company!" snorted Paul, nearly spilling his beer. "Hey, the other night I caught that blonde bitch douching with Gravy Train."

•

Two girls were strolling down the street when the redhead exclaimed, "Oh, how sad—a dead bird."

The blonde looked up and said, "Where?"

•

Why do blondes wear shoulder pads?

So they won't hurt themselves when they go, "I dunno, I dunno." *[Shake head vigorously from side to side.]*

•

So how do you kill a blonde?

Put spikes in her shoulder pads.

•

What else does a blonde say after sex?

"Thanks, guys."

•

Coming into the bar, Joe quickly picked out an adorable blonde, sat down next to her, and pulled a frog out of his pocket. Flashing his winning smile, Joe informed her that it was a very special frog. "His name's Bucky."

"Oh, wow! Really?" said the blonde, flashing a big smile. "What's so special about him?"

Blushing a bit, Joe confessed he was embarrassed to tell her. But the girl was very curious, so finally he whispered, "This frog can eat pussy."

The girl slapped him so hard he fell off his barstool, calling him a crude, filthy liar. "Hey dude, I'm not one of those dumb blondes who falls for any silly line she hears, you know!"

But Joe kept assuring her that it was no lie. In fact, it wasn't even an exaggeration. And after much discussion and quite a few Brandy Alexanders, the luscious blonde agreed to come back to his suite to see the frog in action. After she'd spread her lovely long legs, Joe positioned the frog appropriately and commanded, "Okay, Bucky, do your stuff!"

But despite his owner's repeated exhortations, the frog remained completely immobile, betraying no interest at all in the delightful prospect before him. Finally Joe sighed deeply, picked up the frog, and said, "Bucky . . . I'm only going to show you one more time."

•

Why are the Japanese so smart?
    No blondes.

•

How do you know if a blonde has been making chocolate chip cookies?

There're M&M shells all over the floor.

•

How do you put sparkle in a blonde's eyes?

Shine a flashlight in her ear.

•

Jeff couldn't wait to get the beautiful blonde to go to bed with him. It wasn't long before they were going at it hot and heavy, and he couldn't help noticing that with each thrust of his pelvis, his partner's toes would curl up. A while later they took a shower and ended up screwing again, and this time her toes stayed flat. Puzzled, he whispered in her ear, "How come when we do it in bed your toes go up, and in the shower they don't?"

"You silly goose," replied the blonde with a giggle. "Because I take my pantyhose off in the shower!"

•

What's the difference between a blonde and a 747?
  Not everyone's been on a 747.

•

The two beautiful blonde Swedish girls decided to tour the United States, beginning their trip in New York City. Spotting a hot-dog vendor in the street, Erna wondered out loud, "Do they eat dogs in America?"
  Her companion shrugged. "I don't really know."
  "Well, we might as well get used to the food here," Erna pointed out, so they each bought a hot dog and sat down on a nearby park bench. Unwrapping the wax paper, Birgit inspected her lunch, turned to her friend, and asked, "What part did you get?"

•

What does a blonde say after you blow in her ear?
  "Thanks for the refill."

•

What does a bleached blonde have in common with a 747?

They both have a black box.

•

The horny blonde goes to the supermarket and gets all hot and bothered eyeing the carrots and cucumbers. By the time she gets to the checkout line she can't hold out much longer, so she asks one of the supermarket baggers to carry her groceries out to the car for her. They're halfway across the lot when the blonde slips her hand down his pants and whispers, "You know, I've got an itchy pussy."

"Sorry, lady," says the bagger, "but I can't tell one of those Japanese cars from another."

•

What's the difference between a blonde and a bowling ball?

You can only fit three fingers in a bowling ball.

•

What do you call a brunette between two blondes?
An interpreter.

•

The young blonde bride made her first appointment with a gynecologist, drove in from the isolated homestead, and told him of her and her husband's wish to start a family. "We've been trying for months now, Doctor Keith, and I don't seem to be able to get pregnant," she confessed miserably.

"I'm sure we'll solve the problem," the doctor reassured her. "If you'll just get up on the examining table and take off your underpants . . ."

"Well, all right, Doctor," agreed the naive blonde, blushing, "but I'd rather have my husband's baby."

•

What's a blonde's mating call?
"I'm sooooo drunk."

•

What's another blonde mating call?
  "Next."

•

What's a brunette's mating call?
  "Is that blonde bitch gone yet?"

•

A prosperous stockbroker married a gorgeous blonde and had everything money could buy, until he gambled on a few bad tips and lost everything. He came home with a heavy heart that night and said to his wife, "You better learn to cook, Bibi, so we can fire the chef."

The blonde thought it over for a few moments and said, "Okay, but you better learn to screw, George, so we can fire the chauffeur."

•

Why does it say TGIF on a blonde's bra?
  Instructions: Tits Go In First.

●

And why does it say TGIF on her socks?
  Toes Go In First.

●

What's the first thing a blonde does in the morning?
  Introduce herself.

●

Jack was desperate to get Lila to marry him, but right after the wedding his ardor cooled, and pretty soon the little blonde was feeling awfully neglected. When she confided in her next-door neighbor, the woman suggested that she start ordering her milk from the milkman. "He's a good-looking young guy, and I bet he won't mind settling the bill with some sex."

Lila took her advice, and sure enough, when the milk-man presented his bill he was delighted to settle for a long and energetic screw. Pulling his overalls back on, he reached for the bill to mark it "Paid."

"No way, dude!" cried the blonde, grabbing it out of his hand. "You brought me this milk a quart at a time, and that's the way I'm going to pay for it."

•

Why did the blonde return her vibrator to the department store?

It chipped her teeth.

•

What do you call a blonde who's dyed her hair brown?

Artificial intelligence.

•

How do you keep a blonde busy for hours?
  Give her a bag of M&Ms to alphabetize.

•

Know where a blonde can always find a job?
  Proofreading at the M&M factory.

•

Why did the M&M foreman have to fire the blonde?
  She was eating all the W's.

•

The horny blonde confessed her embarrassing predica-
ment: she had gotten her vibrator stuck inside her.
  "Don't worry, we'll have it out in no time," the gyne-
cologist reassured her.
  "No way, hang on a sec!" she cried.
  "Well, what on earth are you here for?" he asked,
puzzled.
  "Could you please change the batteries?"

How is a blonde like a turtle?
   Get her on her back and she's screwed.

What have you got when you line up ten blondes ear to ear?
   A wind tunnel.

How do you get a blonde to marry you?
   Tell her she's pregnant.

Why don't blondes wear hoop earrings?
   Their high heels keep getting stuck in them.

Why do blondes wash their hair in the kitchen sink?
  That's where you clean vegetables, isn't it?

A certain virginal and shy college freshman was lucky to have a roommate who was considerably more experienced. When the bashful boy broke down and explained his predicament, his roommate was quick to offer to set him up with a blonde who'd made the rounds of the campus. "Just take this bimbo out to dinner and a show, and then let nature take its course," he explained reassuringly. "This girl knows what the score is, and she's even a natural blonde."

The roommate arranged the date as promised. The freshman was delighted by his cute, outgoing companion, and they spent the evening dining and dancing. On the way home he parked his car in a dark lane, broke out in a cold sweat, and blurted out, "Gosh, I sure would love to have a little pussy."

"I would too," sighed the blonde. "Mine's the size of a milk pail."

How do you drown a blonde?
    Put a mirror at the bottom of a swimming pool.

•

What's another way to drown a blonde?
    Put a scratch 'n' sniff at the bottom of the bathtub.

•

A young country girl came to town for a day. She was window shopping when a beautiful pair of red shoes caught her eye, and as she stood admiring them the clerk came out, eyed her long blonde hair and ample curves, and asked if he could help her. The girl admitted that she'd spent all her money but that she'd do anything to get her hands on those red shoes.

The clerk thought it over for a moment. "I think we can work out a deal," he told her. "Go lie down on the couch in the back room." Soon he came in and closed the door. "So do you want those shoes bad enough to put out for them?" he asked. When she nodded he pulled down his pants, exposing a hard-on about nine inches long. "Honey, I'll screw you with this big cock of mine until you squirm with pleasure and scream in ecstasy and go wild with desire."

"Fer sure," agreed the blonde, fondling the shoes. She spread her legs and lay back cheerfully. Sure she couldn't last long, the salesman started pumping away, but she lay there like a dishrag. Pretty soon he'd come twice and begun to worry about getting soft, so he started going at it for all he was worth. Sure enough he felt her arms go around his neck and her legs tighten around his waist. "Best fuck you've ever had, right?" chortled the man. "In a couple of seconds you'll be coming like crazy."

"Oh, no, silly, it's not that," said the blonde. "I'm just trying on my new shoes."

•

Why don't blondes eat pickles?
    Because their heads get stuck in the jar.

•

Why don't blondes make Kool-Aid?
    They can't fit eight cups of water into that little packet.

How do you give a blonde a brain transplant?
Blow in her ear.

⏺

On the way back from a ski trip, the bus went over an embankment and four women—three brunettes and one blonde—were instantly killed. They materialized at the Pearly Gates, where St. Peter asked the first brunette whether she had performed any unclean acts during her time on earth. Blushing, she confessed to having kissed a boy.

"Wash your lips in the holy water," ordered St. Peter, "and proceed into Heaven. And you, miss, have you sinned?"

The second brunette blushed deeply and stammered, "St. Peter, I once touched a man's penis."

"Wash your hands in the holy water and you shall be cleansed and admitted into Heaven." He turned around expectantly, only to be startled by the sight of both women fighting for position in front of the font of holy water. "Ladies, ladies," he remonstrated. "What in Heaven's name is going on?"

"It's like this, St. Peter," replied the third brunette. "I was last in line, but don't you think I should be allowed to gargle in the holy water before that blonde bitch has to sit in it?"

•

What do blondes and beer bottles have in common?
  They're both empty from the neck up.

•

What do you call a group of blondes in the freezer?
  Frosted Flakes.

•

Why don't blondes get coffee breaks?
  It takes too long to retrain them.

•

When Wendy won the lottery everyone agreed that it couldn't have happened to a nicer gal. And indeed the first thing the bighearted blonde announced that she was going to do with the money was build three swimming pools for her friends to use.

"Why three?" asked the *Daily News* reporter.

"One with cold water that'll be really refreshing, one heated to eighty degrees for folks that like the water warm, and one empty."

"Empty?" pursued the reporter.

"Sure," explained Wendy. "Some of my friends can't swim."

•

What do you call a zit on a blonde's butt?

A brain tumor.

•

What do you do when a militant blonde feminist throws a grenade at you?

Pull out the pin and throw it back.

The three blondes went on vacation together, and to save money they shared the same hotel room. But three women in a double bed didn't make for very comfortable sleeping quarters, so Sherry gave up and moved onto the rug.

She was just about asleep when her girlfriend shook her by the shoulder. "You might as well get back in bed, Sherry—there's lots of room now."

●

Why did the blonde trim her favorite skirt with fur?
To keep the back of her neck warm.

●

How do you make a blonde laugh on Monday?
Tell her a joke on Friday.

●

Why do blondes have crow's feet?
From squinting and saying, "Suck *what*? Oh, okay."

•

Did you hear about the two blondes who went for a walk and got into an argument? One insisted the tracks underfoot were deer tracks.

"No way," insisted the other blonde. "These are definitely moose tracks."

They were still arguing when the train hit them.

•

What does a blonde do after sex?
Walks home.

•

What does it say behind a blonde's ear?
"Inflate to 30 psi."

How can you tell when a blonde is stressed?

There's a tampon behind her ear, and God knows where her pencil is.

⦁

The seventy-five-year-old blonde walked into a bar with a pigeon on her head and shouted, "Whoever can guess the weight of this bird can fuck me!"

Way in the back of the bar, a drunk yelled, "One thousand pounds!"

"Close enough," the blonde responded cheerfully.

⦁

What does a blonde put behind her ears to attract men?

Her legs.

⦁

What are three things blondes and sheep have in common?

They're always in the mood.

They never have a headache.

When you're done screwing them, you toss them out the door.

•

What do blondes and screen doors have in common?

The harder you bang them, the looser they get.

•

A dumb blonde, a smart blonde, and Santa Claus are walking down the street and see a twenty-dollar bill lying on the sidewalk. Guess who picks it up?

The dumb blonde—the other two don't exist.

•

Harry noticed he was running low on rubbers, so he stopped by the local drug store. "What size?" asked the pharmacist's assistant sweetly.

When he admitted he wasn't sure of his size, the cute blonde led him into the back room, lifted her skirt, and told him to enter her. He was delighted to oblige.

"Size six," she informed him after a moment or two. "Now take it out. How many, please?"

Harry bought a dozen, and on the way down the street he ran into his friend Alan, to whom he eagerly recounted the whole episode. Needless to say, Alan rushed right in to place an order. "I'm afraid I don't know my size," he told the salesgirl.

So the blonde led him into the back room and repeated the procedure. "Size seven sir, now take it out. How many, please?"

But Alan plugged away, undeterred, until he came. "None, thanks," he told her, zipping up his fly and smiling broadly. "Just came in for a fitting."

•

What did the blonde say when the doctor told her she was pregnant?

"Are you sure it's mine?"

•

Why did the blonde climb over the chain-link fence?
  To see what was on the other side.

·

What do you call twenty blondes in a circle?
  A dope ring.

·

The blonde private had joined the Army Airborne with dreams of parachuting, but now that the moment had come for her first jump, she was pretty scared. The instructor assured her that all she had to do was count to ten and pull the cord. "Relax—even if your chute malfunctions, the reserve will open automatically. And our truck will be waiting for you at the drop site." With those comforting words, the instructor gave Brenda a shove, and she found herself plummeting towards the earth.

After a few seconds of pure terror, the private began counting, and pulled the ripcord right on time. Nothing happened. Trying to stay calm, Brenda waited for the reserve chute to open. Nothing happened. "Shit," she muttered as the ground rushed towards her, "I'll just bet the truck isn't there either."

What's the difference between an intelligent blonde and Bigfoot?
　　Bigfoot's been sighted.

•

Why did the blonde resolve to have only three children?
　　Because she read that one of every four children born in the world is Chinese.

•

Why were blondes given bigger brains than dogs?
　　So they wouldn't hump men's legs at cocktail parties.

•

The beautiful blonde babe was complaining to her best friend about the way men just took for granted that she'd go to bed with them. "I went over to this guy's apartment last night, and he just *assumed* I was going to spend the night," she recounted. "I was so insulted I put my dress back on and left!"

•

Why does the blonde always take a quarter along on her dates?
   So that if she can't come she can call.

•

Why did the blonde lose her job at the pharmacy?
   She kept trying to fit the little bottles in her typewriter.

•

Why do little blonde girls put fish in their underwear?
   So they can smell like big blonde girls.

What's a blonde 10?

One who sucks and fucks till midnight and then turns into a pizza and a six-pack.

•

The two blondes ran into each other one Friday night. "Guess what?" asked Dawn with a smirk. "My boyfriend came home with a dozen roses. Now I'm going to have to spend all weekend with my legs in the air."

"Gee, Dawn, how come?" wondered Shirley. "Don't you have a vase?"

•

What's a beaten, bloody body lying in a ditch by the side of the road?

A brunette who's told too many blonde jokes.

•

A fellow met a friendly blonde at a party and was dying to get into her pants. She seemed willing and he couldn't wait, so the minute he got her alone he jumped on top of her and they started doing it. "If I'd known you were a virgin," the fellow commented afterwards, "I'd have taken my time."

"If I'd known you had time," she tittered, "I'd have taken off my pantyhose."

•

Did you hear about the blonde hoodlum?
    She spray-paints her name on chain-link fences.

•

What do you get when you cross a blonde and a Chinese person?
    Someone who'll suck your laundry.

•

Some time after his wife of thirty years had died, Leonard decided that he'd like to remarry. Soon afterward he met a sweet blonde thing named Lorna and proposed to her.

Lorna laid it on the line. "Leonard," she said, "there are some things I'm not prepared to live without if I marry you. First of all, I need a condominium in Florida."

"No problem. I've got a gorgeous condo in St. Pete," said the old man.

"Also, I need my own bathroom."

"Two and a half baths at my house—you get your choice."

Then Lorna looked Leonard straight in the eye. "And sex?"

"Infrequently," answered the old man.

Thinking it over, the blonde asked, "Is that one word or two?"

●

If Tarzan and Jane were blonde, what would Cheetah be?

A fur coat.

●

What's a blonde's idea of natural childbirth?
    Absolutely no make-up.

·

Did you hear about the abortion clinic that offers blondes a discount?
    There's a year-long waiting list.

·

What did the blonde do when she learned that ninety percent of all driving accidents occur within ten miles of the home?
    She moved.

·

A blonde was having a sandwich at the corner luncheonette when she was approached by a small man dressed all in green. "Know what?" asked the odd little fellow in a confidential tone. "I'm a leprechaun, and I'm feeling extremely generous. So generous, in fact, that I'm willing to grant you any three wishes you'd like."

"No kidding! Gee, that's great," blurted the lucky girl. "I could sure use some extra cash."

"No problem," said the leprechaun with a gracious wave. "The trunk of your car is now crammed with hundred-dollar bills. What's next?"

"Well, I wouldn't mind moving to a nicer apartment."

"Consider it done," announced the leprechaun grandly. "You now have the keys to a two thousand-square-foot penthouse condominium on Park Avenue. And your third wish?"

"Well, uh, how about a gorgeous boyfriend?" suggested the blonde, blushing a bit.

"He's waiting for you in the bedroom of your new condominium, built like a god and hung like a horse."

"Wow, this is really great," said the lucky girl, getting down from her stool and starting for the door. "I wish there were some way to thank you."

"Oh, but there is," spoke up the man in green. "I'd like a blow job."

"A blow job?" She wasn't sure she'd heard right.

"Yup. And after all I've given you, it doesn't seem like much to ask, now does it?"

The blonde had to admit this was true, so in a dark corner of the bar she vigorously obliged her benefactor. As she pulled on her jacket and turned away, the man in green tugged on her sleeve. "Just one question," he asked. "How old are you?"

"Twenty-eight."

"And you still believe in leprechauns?"

Hear about the blonde who wanted to trade her menstrual cycle . . .

. . . for a Honda?

•

Then there was the blonde who said she'd do anything for a fur coat . . .

. . . and now she can't button it over her belly.

•

The blonde was so hungry on her way home that she stopped in at a pizzeria. When her pizza came out of the oven, the guy asked her if she'd like it cut into four or eight pieces.

"Make it four," she answered, after scratching her head for a minute. "I'll never be able to eat eight."

•

What did the blonde English major think Moby Dick was?

A venereal disease.

•

Two blondes were sunning themselves in the backyard one day. When Loni got up to get a soda, her friend Sherri noticed she was walking rather oddly, feet set wide apart. "Why're you walking so funny?" she asked. "Is something wrong?"

"Heck no," replied Loni. "I've got a big date tonight, so my hair's in curlers."

•

Why do so few blondes breast-feed their babies?

It hurts too much when they boil the nipples.

•

Why do blondes have two sets of lips?

So they can piss and moan at the same time.

•

Did you hear about the blonde who thought a sanitary belt was a drink from a clean shot glass?

•

The divorce was an especially nasty one, as the woman was suing on the grounds that her husband had completely failed to satisfy her. "Well, Your Honor," the gorgeous blonde informed the court in a stage whisper, "His weenie was so teeny—I'm talkin' *teeny*—that it wasn't even worth the effort."

The sympathetic judge awarded her a substantial cash settlement, and on her way out of the courtroom she walked past her ex-husband and hissed, "So long, sucker."

Beside himself with fury, he stuck a finger in each corner of his mouth, stretched it as wide as possible, and retorted, "So long, bitch."

•

Did you hear about the blonde bride who was so horny, she carried a bouquet of batteries?

•

What's a blonde's idea of dental floss?
   Pubic hair.

•

The blonde was pulled over in her Corvette for speeding and taken down to police headquarters. Taking one look at her, the desk sergeant stood up and unzipped his fly.
   "Oh, no," cried the blonde repentantly. "Not another breathalyzer test!"

•

Did you hear about the blonde prisoner who was found unconscious in her jail cell with twelve bumps on her head?

She tried to hang herself with a rubber band.

•

What did the blonde do when her doctor informed her he'd found sugar in her urine?

Peed on her cornflakes.

•

Little Janie went off to public school and came home full of questions. "Mommy, how did baby Brendan next door get born?" she asked.

"The stork brought him, honey," was her mother's prim reply. "Want to help me bake some cookies?"

"Nah. Mommy, so how did the twins in the corner house get born?"

"The stork just carried two babies at once, sweetie."

"Damn," muttered the little blonde with a scowl. "Doesn't anyone in this neighborhood fuck?"

•

Did you hear about the sophisticated blonde?
  She thought her period was French Provincial.

•

Know what a "fuck-off" is?
  The tie-breaker at an all-blonde beauty contest.

•

There are three women on the fast track in a particular corporation. The president realizes it's time to promote one of them, but he can't decide whom to choose. So he devises a little test. One day while all three are out at lunch, he places five hundred dollars on each of their desks.
  #1 returns the money to him immediately.
  #2 pockets the cash.
  #3 invests in the market and returns fifteen hundred dollars to him the next morning.
  So who gets the promotion?
  The blonde with the big tits!

What do fat blondes and mopeds have in common?
    They're both fun to ride until a friend sees you.

•

Why are blondes giving up bowling for screwing?
    The balls are lighter, and you don't have to change your shoes.

•

Tim was thrilled when his gorgeous blonde girlfriend agreed to marry him, and both promptly made appointments with the doctor for their physicals. A few days later the doctor called Tim in and told him he had some good news and some bad news. "The good news," he went on, "is that your fiancée has gonorrhea."

    Tim paled. "If that's the *good* news, Doctor, then what the hell's next?"

    "She didn't get it from you."

What's that white stuff you find in a blonde's panties?
  Clitty litter.

How is a blonde like an oven?
  They're both easy to heat up so you can stick the meat in.

What's the function of a bellybutton?
  It gives a blonde somewhere to put her gum on the way down.

All her life Sally Pritchett had dreamed of being a teacher, and sure enough, one day she faced her own class of third-graders. The sweet blonde thing decided to start out with a vocabulary quiz, and instructed the children to think of a three-syllable word and use it in a sentence. "Yes, Susie?" she prompted, turning to a freckle-faced kid in the front row.

"Beautiful," sighed Susie. "My teacher is beautiful."

"Why, thank you," responded Sally with a smile. "Someone else? Mary?"

"Wonderful. Miss Pritchett is wonderful."

The teacher nodded graciously. "Thank you, Mary. Yes, Teddy?"

"Urinate," said the boy with a grin.

"Teddy!" The teacher was shocked.

"Urinate, but if your tits were bigger, you'd be a ten!"

•

Blonde #1: "This is a little embarrassing, but every time I sneeze I have an orgasm."
Blonde #2: "No kidding. Are you taking anything for it?"
Blonde #1: "Snuff."

•

What's the difference between a blonde and a prostitute?

Prostitutes don't drive Ferraris.

•

How many blondes does it take to change a light bulb?

None. Their boyfriends do it for them.

•

When the blonde called up and asked her pharmacist what to do about her boyfriend's dandruff, he recommended Head & Shoulders.

A week later she dropped by the drug store and asked, "Say, how do you give someone shoulders?"

•

Then she decided her boyfriend needed some deodorant. "Certainly," said the pharmacist. "How about the ball type?"

"Oh, no," she replied, "it's for under his arms."

•

Did you hear about the blonde who had two chances to get pregnant?

She blew both of them.

•

"Excuse me, could you tell me the time?" asked the blonde of a man at the street corner.

"Sure . . . it's three-fifteen," he replied with a smile.

"Thanks," she said, a puzzled look crossing her face. "You know, it's the weirdest thing—I've been asking that question all day long, and each time I get a different answer."

•

Male secretary: "Feel free to use my Dictaphone."
New blonde employee: "No thanks! I'll use my finger like everyone else."

•

Did you hear about the blonde who got an A.M. radio?

It took her a month to figure out she could play it at night.

•

The blonde was thrilled to land a job as spokesmodel for a cosmetics company which required quite a bit of business travel. She was on a small commuter flight when she happened to catch sight of one of the propellers conking out. A minute later, the pilot calmly announced, "Ladies and gentlemen, this flight will be fifteen minutes late," so she thought nothing more of it.

Ten minutes later a second engine went out. "Ladies and gentlemen, this flight will be forty minutes late."

Pretty soon the blonde looked out her window just in time to see the second propeller on her side of the plane stop spinning, followed by the announcement, "Ladies and gentlemen, this flight will be one hour and twenty minutes late."

"Jeez," muttered the blonde, "if that last engine goes out we'll be up here all day."

•

Why should you suggest "68" to a blonde?
    That's when she goes down on you and you tell her you owe her one.

•

Why did the pregnant blonde lose her job at the sperm bank?
    Her employers discovered she'd been embezzling.

•

How can you tell when a blonde is horny?
    When you put your hand in her pants and it feels like a horse eating oats.

What's the difference between a young blonde and an old blonde?

A young one uses Vaseline; an old one uses Poli-Grip.

●

A blonde walked into a bar and ordered a Michelob Light. It tasted so good that she ordered another, and another, and another, until she passed out cold. Several truck drivers had been watching this progression with interest, and promptly took her into the back room and took turns screwing her.

Early the next morning the woman came to and made her way home, but that night she appeared again, ordered a Michelob Light, and got so drunk that all the truck drivers, along with a few of their buddies, had their way with her again. This went on for several more evenings, until one evening the blonde came in and ordered a Miller Lite.

"Sure thing," said the bartender, "but how come you're switching brands?"

"Michelob makes my pussy hurt," she explained.

●

What's the difference between a dead brunette lying in the road and a dead blonde lying in the road?

There's skid marks in front of the blonde.

•

Did you hear about the blonde who thought intercourse was a state highway?

•

What did the blonde write home from her vacation?

"Hi. Having a great time. Where am I?"

•

How many blondes does it take to start a car?

Five. One to steer, one to work the pedals, two to push, and one to sit under the hood saying, "Va-ROOOM, Va-ROOOM."

Did you know they finally sent a blonde astronaut into space? She had a monkey as co-pilot, and her instructions were to wait for the green light to go on.

The first day in orbit a red light went on, and the monkey took down all the instrument readings. The second day, a red light went on, and the monkey took out its slide rule and made all the appropriate calculations. The third day a green light went on.

"Okay, what do I do now?" asked the blonde.

"Feed the monkey," said Mission Control.

Did you hear about the blonde whose boyfriend said he loved her?

She believed him.

How can you tell which computer terminal belongs to the blonde?

It's got White-Out all over the screen.

Did you hear about the new epidemic among blondes? It's called MAIDS—if they don't get one, they die.

A very experienced blonde changed gynecologists, and she was rather embarrassed when the doctor took a look and commented, "Why, that's the biggest pussy I've ever seen—the biggest pussy I've ever seen!"

"You didn't have to say it twice," she said with a sniff.

"I didn't," responded the doctor.

What did the blind blonde say as she was making love with her new boyfriend?

"Funny, you don't feel Jewish."

Doctor (taking up his stethoscope): "Big breaths."
Adolescent Blonde: "Yeth, and I'm not even thixteen."

•

What was the blonde's complaint about oral sex?
  The lousy view.

•

As the newlywed couple was checking into the hotel for their honeymoon, another couple at the desk offered to show them around the town that night. Thanking them for the kind offer, the bridegroom explained with a wink at his stunning blonde wife that they'd prefer to take a rain check.

When the second couple came down to breakfast the next morning they were astonished to catch sight of the groom alone in the hotel bar, apparently drowning his sorrows. "Why, you should be the happiest man in the world today," they said, coming over to him, "with that gorgeous blonde all yours for life."

"Yesterday I was," said the man mournfully, "but this morning, without realizing it, I put three ten-dollar bills on the pillow and got up to get dressed."

"Hey, cheer up, she probably didn't notice."

"That's the problem," the groom went on. "Without even thinking, she gave me five dollars change."

•

What happened when the blonde got locked in the car?
  Her blond boyfriend had to use a coathanger to get her out.

•

Did you hear about the blonde lesbian?
  She likes men.

•

Fred came home from work in time to catch his blonde girlfriend sliding naked down the bannister. "What the hell are you doing?" he demanded.
  "Just heating up dinner, darling," she cried cheerfully.

A man and his girlfriend were fooling around when the blonde asked, "Honey, could you take your ring off? It's hurting me."

"Ring, hell," he snorted. "That's my wrist watch."

•

What's the definition of a metallurgist?

A man who can tell if a platinum blonde is a virgin metal or a common ore.

•

Why did the blonde with the huge pussy douche with Crest?

She heard it reduces cavities.

•

One night Fred came home from work and told his wife that he had just signed up with the company hockey team. Worried that he might hurt himself, his wife went out the next day to buy him a cup.

The middle-aged blonde sales clerk showed her the selection, and told her there was a range of sizes.

"Gee, I'm really not sure what Fred's size is," confessed his wife. The saleswoman helpfully extended her pinkie.

"No, it's bigger than that."

She extended a second finger.

"Nope, bigger than that," said the wife.

A third finger.

"Still bigger," she said, blushing slightly.

When the clerk extended her thumb as well, she said, "Yes, that's about right."

So the blonde put all five fingers in her mouth, pulled them out, and announced expertly, "That's a medium."

•

What did the South African blonde give her boyfriend?
  Apart-head.

•

What was the blonde surgeon's claim to fame?
   She performed the world's first successful hemorrhoid transplant.

●

Why did the blonde hippie take two hits of LSD?
   She wanted to go on a round trip.

●

Blonde #1: "Have you ever read Shakespeare?"
Blonde #2: "No, who wrote it?"

●

Hear about the blonde mom who put an ice pack on her chest to keep the milk fresh?

●

Two girlfriends were speeding down the highway at well over ninety miles an hour. "Hey," asked the brunette at the wheel, "see any cops following us?"

The blonde turned around for a long look. "As a matter of fact, I do."

"Shit," cursed the brunette. "Are his flashers on?"

The blonde turned around again. "Yup . . . nope . . . yup . . . nope . . . yup. . . ."

•

Why did the blonde blow her lover after sex?
She wanted to have her cock and eat it too.

•

Did you hear the new slogan for Clairol?
"Buy a double batch and get a snatch to match!"

•

Did you hear about the blonde with a degree in psychology?

She'll blow your mind, too.

•

Vanna had two passions: she loved shopping, and she hated wearing underwear. One day she went looking for a new pair of shoes, and since she was wearing a skirt the salesman was enjoying an excellent view. After the third or fourth pair of shoes, the guy couldn't stand watching the cute blonde from the sidelines one minute longer. "Lady," he said, "that's some beautiful sight. I could eat that pussy full of ice cream."

Disgusted, Vanna stalked out of the store, called her boyfriend to tell him about the incident, and asked him to go beat the shit out of the salesman. When he flatly refused, the little blonde asked why.

"Three reasons," the boyfriend replied. "Number one: you shouldn't have been out in a skirt with no underpants. Number two: you have enough shoes to last you ten years. And number three: I don't want to mess with any son of a bitch who can eat that much ice cream."

•

A blonde walked into the corner hardware store, found the hinges she was looking for, and brought them up to the counter.

"Need a screw for those hinges?" asked the proprietor.

"No," she answered after reflecting for a bit, "but how about a blow job for the toaster in the back?"

•

Did you hear about the blonde from Kiev?
She gives glow jobs.

•

How does a bitchy blonde do it doggie-style?
First she takes her clothes off and then she makes her husband roll over and beg.

•

"I hope you can help me, Doc," said the blonde to the podiatrist. "My feet hurt me all the time."

The doctor asked her to walk down the hall and back while he observed, and when she sat back down he pointed out that she was extremely bowlegged. "Do you know if this is a congenital problem?"

"Oh no, it's my feet that are bothering me, not my genitals," said the blonde with a giggle. "Though I've been screwing doggie fashion a lot."

"Well, I'd recommend trying another sexual position," said the doctor, slightly taken aback.

"No way," replied the blonde tartly. "That's the only way my Doberman likes it."

•

Why was the blonde snorting Nutri-Sweet?
    She thought it was diet coke.

•

Know why most blonde jokes are so short?
    So other blondes can get them too.

How can you tell a blonde who's really conceited?
  She screams her own name when she comes.

"The man next to me is jerking off!" hissed the blonde
to her girlfriend as they sat in the darkened movie the-
ater.
  "Just ignore him," her friend suggested.
  "I can't," moaned the blonde. "He's using my hand."

What happens when a blonde puts her panties on back-
wards?
  She gets her ass chewed out.

What did the really dumb blonde say when someone blew in her bra?

"Thanks for the refill."

•

Why don't blondes like the 65 mph speed limit?

Because at 69 they get to blow a rod.

•

A blonde goes into a bar and sits down. The bartender asks what she'd like to drink and she says, "Bring me a beer."

"Anheuser-Busch?" asks the bartender.

"Just fine, thanks," she answers, "and how's yer cock?"

•

Why don't blondes drink beer on the beach?

They're afraid they'll get sand in their Schlitz.

What's the ultimate in embarrassment for a blonde?

When her Ben-Wa balls set off the metal detector at the airport.

＊

A certain couple fell on really hard times, and since the husband already worked full-time and part of a night shift, they decided the only way to keep the family afloat was for his cute blonde wife to go out and sell herself.

One night she didn't return until the wee hours, disheveled and exhausted. Watching her flop onto the sofa like a limp dishrag, her husband said sympathetically, "You look like you've really had a rough night, honey."

"I sure have," she gasped.

"Well, did you make a lot of money, at least?" he asked.

His wife managed a proud smile. "One hundred and thirty dollars and twenty-five cents."

"Twenty-five cents!" exclaimed the husband. "Who was the cheap bastard who only gave you two bits?"

"Why," said the surprised blonde, *"all* of them."

＊

What's six inches long, has a bald head on it, and drives blondes wild?
A hundred-dollar bill.

•

Why do blondes like tilt steering wheels?
More head room.

•

What do blondes and computers have in common?
You realize you never really appreciated them until they go down on you.

•

Edith and Roberta were hanging out their laundry in their backyards when the talk came around to why Marcia's laundry never got rained on. So when their beautiful blonde neighbor came out with her laundry basket, Roberta asked Marcia how come she always seemed to know in advance whether it was going to rain. "Your laundry's never hanging out on those days," she commented in an aggrieved tone.

Marcia leaned over her fence and winked at the two homely brunettes. "When I wake up in the morning I look over at Buddy," she explained. "If his penis is hanging over his right leg, I know it's going to be fair weather and I come right out with my laundry. On the other hand, if it's hanging left, for sure it's going to rain, so I hang it up inside."

"Well, smarty-pants," said Edith, "what's the forecast if Buddy's got a hard-on?"

"Honey," replied the blonde with a smile, "on a day like *that* you don't do the *laundry.*"

●

What do blondes and dogshit have in common?
    The older they get, the easier they are to pick up.

●

Walking down a deserted street one day, the aging blonde was accosted by a determined thief. "I'm telling you the truth, I don't have any money," she pleaded, but the mugger wouldn't believe her and started to feel around her bra for a possible hiding place.

"Young man," she cooed after another minute or two, "I told you I don't have any money—but if you keep that up, I'll write you a check."

●

The man rolled over in bed and asked his new lover, "Do you smoke after sex?"

"I dunno," admitted the blonde, sitting up. "I never looked."

●

How do you brainwash a blonde?
Step on her douche bag.

●

What did the blonde do when she found out she was pregnant with triplets?

Went looking for the three guys.

•

One day the blonde came home and told her mother that she'd been raped by a large black man.

"Well, hurry, go into the kitchen, cut up a lemon and suck on it," her mother instructed.

"Will that keep me from getting pregnant?" asked the blonde.

"No," snapped her mother, "but it'll wipe that stupid grin off your face."

•

How did the blonde rob the drive-in window at the bank?

She put her gun in the little basket along with a note reading, "This is a stick-up."

•

Why did the blonde return her new scarf?

It was too tight.

•

Milton came into his blonde wife's room one day. "If I were, say, disfigured, would you still love me?" he asked her.

"Darling, I'll always love you," she said calmly, filing her nails.

"How about if I became impotent, couldn't make love to you anymore?" he asked anxiously.

"Don't worry, darling, I'll always love you," she told him, buffing her nails.

"Well, how about if I lost my job as Vice-President?" Milton went on. "If I weren't pulling in six figures anymore? Would you still love me then?"

The blonde looked up into her husband's worried face. "Milton, I'll always love you," she reassured him, "but most of all, I'll really miss you."

•

Why do blondes have such big tits and tight pussies?

Because men have such big mouths and little peckers.

•

How is a blonde like a bank?
   She loses interest when you withdraw your assets.

•

What's a blonde's dilemma?
   Meeting a guy with herpes and a big dick.

•

How did the blonde keep from getting raped?
   She beat off her attacker.

•

The night before her wedding, Angie pulled her mother aside for an intimate little chat. "Mom," she confided,

"I want you to tell me how I can make my new husband happy."

The bride's mother sat down on the bed next to the sweet blonde thing and took a deep breath. "Well, my child," she began, "when two people love, honor, and respect each other, love can be a very beautiful thing."

"I know how to fuck, Mom," interrupted the girl. "I want you to teach me how to make macaroni and cheese."

•

How did the blonde prove that women enjoy sex more than men?

She said, "When your ear itches and you put your little finger in and wiggle it around and take it out again, what feels better, your finger or your ear?"

•

What do you call a blonde who gave an airplane passenger a hand job?

A highjacker.

•

How do blondes part their hair?
   In the middle. *[Spread your legs.]*

•

Hear about the blonde who went to the beach?
   She was asked to leave the area after the lifeguard caught her going down for the third time.

•

How can you tell if a blonde is paranoid?
   She puts a condom on her vibrator.

•

What do you call pulling off a blonde's pantyhose?
   Foreplay.

An amateur golfer playing in his first tournament was delighted when a beautiful blonde came up to him after the round and suggested he come over to her place. The fellow was a bit embarrassed to explain that he really couldn't stay all night but that he'd be glad to come over for a while. Twenty minutes later they were in her bed making love. And when it was over, he got out of bed and started getting dressed.

"Hey," called the girl from beneath the covers, "where do you think you're going? Arnold Palmer wouldn't leave so early."

At that the golfer stripped off his clothes and jumped on top of her. Once they'd made love a second time, he got up again and put his pants back on.

"What're you up to?" she asked. "Jack Nicklaus wouldn't think of leaving now." So the golfer pulled off his pants and screwed her a third time, and afterwards he started getting dressed.

"C'mon, you can't leave yet," protested the blonde. "Lee Trevino wouldn't call it a day."

"Lady, would you just tell me one thing?" asked the golfer, looking at her very seriously. "What's par for this hole?"

What do you call three blondes in bed together?
  A menage à twat.

●

What do you call a beautiful, big-breasted blonde lesbian?
  Bitch.

●

Why did the blonde put a condom on each ear?
  She didn't want to get hearing AIDS.

(Know how you get hearing AIDS? From listening to assholes.)

●

What do you have when you sign up a tall blonde **and** two short brunettes for your football team?
  One wide receiver and two tight ends.

What do you get when you cross an elephant and a blonde?

A three-quarter-ton pick-up.

•

When her two pet bunnies died, the blonde was very upset, and so she would always have something to remember them by, she took them to the taxidermist and asked that they both be stuffed.

"No problem," the taxidermist assured her. "And do you want them mounted?"

The blonde considered this for a minute. "No," she decided, "just holding hands."

•

How many blondes does it take to make popcorn?

Four. One to hold the pot, and three to shake the stove.

A blonde, a redhead, and a brunette died and went up to the Pearly Gates, where they were instructed by St. Peter to take off their shirts for religious purposes. "Now, why is it that you have an 'H' on your chest?" he asked the brunette.

Blushing a bit, she explained, "Because whenever my husband made love to me, he wore his Hamilton sweatshirt."

"And why is there a big 'A' on your chest?" St. Peter asked the next woman.

"My husband always wore his Amherst sweatshirt when he was in the mood," the redhead explained coyly.

"And you? Let me guess," said the saint, turning to the third woman and noting the "M" on her chest. "Every time your husband made love to you, he wore his Michigan sweatshirt, right?"

"No, silly," snickered the blonde. "He went to Wisconsin."

•

Hear about the uptight blonde who attended her first orgy?

Now she doesn't know whom to thank.

Why is a convict before sentencing like an inexperienced blonde?

They both know it'll be hard, but they don't know for how long.

●

Why do dogs stick their noses in blondes' crotches?

Because they can.

●

The blonde came home early from work one day and found her boyfriend in bed with the cute girl who lived down the hall. "What the hell is going on here?" she screamed in outrage.

"See," said the boyfriend, turning to his lover, "I *told* you she's an idiot."

●

Did you hear about the blonde who bought an exercise bike and died the very same day?

She tried to ride it home.

•

What's a blond guy's definition of S&M?

Tying the woman's legs together.

•

Then there was the blonde mom who decided it was time for her son to learn to play baseball, so off she went to the sporting-goods store. "How much is this baseball glove?" she asked the salesman.

"Twenty dollars."

"And the bat?"

"Ten dollars."

"I'll take the bat."

"How about a ball for the bat?" suggested the salesman hopefully.

"Nope," answered the blonde thoughtfully, "but I'll blow you for the glove."

Why does it take so long for a blonde baby to be born?
  She's looking for a flashlight.

Why did the blonde lose her job as an elevator operator?
  She couldn't learn the route.

What's a blonde's greatest fear?
  Waking up asleep.

How many blondes does it take to milk a cow?
  Nine. Four to hold the udders, four to hold the legs,

and one to tell them when to move the cow up and down.

•

Know why blondes never dial 911 in an emergency?
   Because they can't find eleven on their telephones.

•

Hear about the blonde who decided to make pineapple upside-down cake to impress her dinner guests?
   First she turned over the oven . . .

•

Why did the blonde sit in a tree?
   So she could call herself a branch manager.

•

Did you hear about the two blonde cowgirls who couldn't tell their horses apart? First they put a hat on one, but it fell off. Then they clipped the tail of the other, but that stopped working as soon as the tail grew back. So finally they put the white horse in one stall and the black one in another.

•

What's this? *[Put your hand in front of your face and move your head rapidly from side to side.]*
   A blonde fanning herself.

•

Did you hear about the pregnant blonde who drove to the supermarket when she went into labor?
   She'd heard they had free delivery.

•

The blonde was explaining her livelihood to a girlfriend. "I put one stocking on my left leg. Then I put another stocking on my right leg. And between the two . . . I make a living."

•

Forced by bad weather to stop over in a seedy town's only hotel, the businessman decided to put his time to good use. "Do you keep stationery?" he asked the blonde at the front desk.

"Yeah," she answered, "until someone touches my clit. Then I go fuckin' crazy."

•

The blonde waitress had scheduled an appointment after work with her gynecologist, and the doctor was quite taken aback when he came across a tea bag in the course of his examination.

"Oh shit," said the waitress when the doctor held it up for her examination. "I wonder what I served my last customer . . ."

How can you spot a disadvantaged blonde?
She's driving a domestic car.

•

What did one blind blonde keep asking the other one?
"Are your tits bigger than mine?"

•

Soon after their honeymoon, the new husband found himself at the doctor's office, where he complained of exhaustion and fatigue. After a thorough examination, the doctor reassured him that there was no organic reason for his complaints.

"However, it's not at all uncommon for young people to wear themselves out in the first weeks or months of married life," he reassured the young fellow with a wink. "What you need is rest. So for the next month, confine your sexual activity to those days of the week with an 'r' in them. That's Thursday, Friday, and Saturday," he went on, "and you'll be feeling up to snuff in no time."

Since the end of the week was approaching, the couple had no problem following the doctor's advice. But on the first scheduled night off, the new bride found herself increasingly restless and horny. Tossing and turning into the wee hours, the horny young blonde finally turned to her husband and shook him awake.

Groggy and bewildered, he mumbled, "What's wrong, baby? What day is it?"

"Mondray," she murmured.

•

How can you find out whether a blonde is ticklish?
Give her two test tickles.

•

What are a blonde's three greatest lies?
1) You're the best.
2) You're the biggest.
3) It doesn't always smell that way.

What do you get when you cross a blonde with a pyromaniac?

The Burning Bush.

•

"Hey, Mick, the usual?" The bartender poured a draft and brought it over to his friend. "What's new?"

"Nothing much," was Mick's reply. "Sally died, though. Remember her? That blowzy blonde widow who lived in the corner house, raised eight kids?" Mick drew on his beer, then said thoughtfully, "Well, at least they're together again."

"Husband and wife, eh?" commiserated the bartender. "That's a nice thought."

"No, no," said Mick brusquely. "Her legs."

•

What chain of food stores do blondes patronize?

Stop 'n' Blow.

Did you hear about the blonde who failed her driver's test three times?

She couldn't learn to sit up in a car.

•

[Note: for this joke you need a long-necked beer bottle as a prop.]

A blonde was out on a date and couldn't seem to come up with anything to talk about but her old boyfriend—his hobbies, his car, his habits. *[Stroke the length of the bottle lovingly during this part of the joke.]*

Finally the new man in her life grew exasperated. "You're always going on about him!" he exploded. "How about thinking about *me* for a change!"

"You've got a point," admitted the blonde. *[Move your hand up to stroke just the neck of the bottle.]* "I'll try."

•

After asking the blonde starlet to strip, why did the producer take off his own clothes?

He wanted to see if she could make it big.

●

The voluptuous blonde was enjoying a stroll around Plato's Retreat, arrogantly examining everyone's equipment before making her choice. In one room she happened upon a scrawny, bald fellow with thick glasses, and to complete the picture, his penis was a puny four inches long.

Checking it out with a sneer, the blonde snickered, "Just who do you think you're going to please with *that?*"

"Me," he answered, looking up with a grin.

●

Did you hear why the blonde failed her driver's test?

When the car stalled, out of habit she jumped into the back seat.

●

Why did the blonde refuse to go down on the guy with the twelve-inch dick?

She didn't want to get foot-in-mouth disease.

•

The blonde came up to the single man at the bar and said boldly, "I cost three hundred dollars—and I'm worth it."

"Is that so?" asked the fellow, looking her over. "Three hundred bucks is a lot of money."

Snuggling up so that he could smell her perfume and leaning over so he could appreciate her cleavage, the blonde proceeded to elaborate upon the skills, the techniques, the talent and imagination she brought to her trade. "I'll make love to you like you've never been made love to before," she promised with a throaty chuckle. "In fact, whisper any three words—picture your wildest fantasy coming true—and I'll make it happen."

"Any three words? For three hundred dollars?" he asked, perking up considerably.

"That's right, baby," confirmed the blonde, blowing him a pouty little kiss.

"We've got a deal," cried the new client happily. He pulled her up onto his lap, pulled her long blonde hair away from her ear, and whispered, "Paint my house."

Why did the blonde drive around the block fifty-seven times?

Her turn signal was stuck.

•

Did you hear about the blonde who broke her leg playing golf?

She fell off the ball wash.

•

When Jackie went to the dentist for the first time in years, she was prepared for bad news. Nevertheless she was a little put out when, after some time, the dentist gasped, "Jesus, what happened to your teeth? They're all gone, and your gums are in terrible shape!"

"If it's such a big problem," retorted the blonde, "then get your face out of my lap."

•

How about the blond kid whose teacher told him to write a hundred-word essay on what he did during summer vacation?

He wrote "Not much" fifty times.

•

Two little blonde girls were walking down the block to school and one said to the other, "Hey, know what I found on the patio the other day? A contraceptive."

"Oh yeah?" said her friend. "What's a patio?"

•

If Tarzan and Jane were blonde, what would Cheetah be?

The smartest of the three.

•

Two young blonde hitchhikers were picked up by a farmer, who motioned to them to sit in the back of his pick-up truck. The girls jumped in and were enjoying the breeze when suddenly a front tire blew, causing the truck to veer off the road and into a pond.

The farmer got out of the cab and swam ashore, where he turned and watched for his two passengers to come to the surface. But as the minutes ticked by he began to lose hope, figuring that they must have drowned. Just as he was turning away, the two girls emerged, sputtering and choking, and made their way to the shore.

"What took you gals so long?" asked the farmer, thumping them on the back. "I figured you for goners."

Still gasping for breath, the blondes explained, "Couldn't get the tailgate down."

•

What do you get when you turn three naked blondes upside-down?

Three brunettes.

•

Why did the blonde name her dog Herpes?

Because it wouldn't heel.

What does a blonde think 7-11 is?

An emergency number.

·

An extremely pale, slight man wearing dark glasses stood out from the usual crowd by the resort pool. Debbi, a middle-aged blonde, immediately settled herself in the deck chair next to his. Introducing herself, she asked, "Why so pale?"

"Leave me alone, lady," grunted the man, "I just got outta jail."

"Oh, I see," said Debbi, pursing her lips. "How long for?"

"Five years."

"That's terrible," she clucked. "For what?"

"Embezzlement."

"Ooh." Debbi nodded knowledgeably.

"And then five years for armed robbery," said the man in a sudden burst of talkativeness, "and then another lousy ten."

"And what was that for?"

"I killed my wife."

A big smile coming over her face, Debbi sat bolt upright. "Tanya," she shouted to her friend across the pool, "he's *single*!"

•

How do blondes count to ten?
  "One, two, three, another, another, another . . ."

•

How did the blind blonde pierce her ear?
  Answering the stapler.

•

What's a blonde's favorite rock group?
  Yes.

•

The new stewardess was summoned to the office of the head of the training program for a severe reprimand. "I heard about that episode on your first flight, Miss Larson," she said, glaring at the voluptuous blonde over the top of her glasses. "From now on, whenever a passenger feels faint, I'll thank you to push his head down between his own legs!"

•

Did you hear about the blonde who accidentally made two dates on the same night?

She managed to squeeze both of them in.

•

What do you call a blonde who relies on the rhythm method of birth control?

Mom.

•

Sam and Cindy grew up next door to each other, and as they grew older, each constantly tried to one-up the other. If Sam got a jungle gym, Cindy got a swing set, and so on, until the contest became a very expensive one for both sets of parents. Finally Sam's father asked what was going on, and when Sam explained it, a big grin came over his face.

Next Saturday Cindy whizzed down the sidewalk on a brand new tricycle. "Nyaah, nyaah," she taunted, tossing her long blonde hair over her shoulder, "look what I've got."

"So?" retorted Sam. "I've got something you'll never have—look!" And he pulled down his pants and showed her.

Realizing she'd been outdone, Cindy ran into her house sobbing. Her father picked her up and tried to comfort her. Getting the whole story out of her, he smiled and whispered something in her ear.

The next day Sam spotted Cindy in the backyard and decided to rub it in. "I've got one of these and you don't," he teased, pulling his pants down again.

"Big deal," said the little blonde haughtily, pulling her skirt up and her underpants down. "My Daddy says that with one of *these* I can have as many of *those* as I want."

•

What would be one of the best things about electing a blonde president?

We wouldn't have to pay her as much!

Rocking with her friends on the front porch, the ninety-two-year-old blonde said proudly, "I've got my health, my heart is strong, my liver is good, and my mind, knock wood . . . Who's there?"

What does a blonde from Malibu wear to a funeral?
  Her black tennis dress.

Why do blondes like to do it doggie style?
  So they can keep watching the Home Shopping Network.

If a bleached blonde and a natural blonde were standing on top of a tower, how could you tell them apart?

A bleached blonde would never throw crumbs to helicopters.

•

Why did the blonde law student fail her bar exam?

She thought an antitrust suit was a chastity belt.

•

A blonde married a Native American, and when their child was born, what do you think they named him?

Running Dumb.

•

Why do blondes have broad shoulders and broad heads?

Because when you ask them a question [shrug your shoulders] they shrug their shoulders, and when you tell them the answer *[slap the top of your head]* they slap the top of their heads and say, "Jeez, now why didn't I think of that?"

•

Did you hear about the first all-blonde space mission? The launch went off without a hitch, they reached orbit, and the first astronaut left the capsule to walk in space. When she knocked on the door to be let back in, the other astronaut asked, "Who's there?"

•

Why did the blonde ask all her friends to save their burned-out light bulbs?

She needed them for the darkroom she was building.

•

"For God's sake, Mindy," said the old woman consolingly to her newly-married neighbor, "why are you crying your eyes out? It can't be that bad."

"My husband's out shooting crap," confessed the blonde with a sob, "and I don't know how to cook it."

•

Did you hear about the blonde who thought a tail assembly . . .

. . . was the company picnic?

•

Did you hear about the blonde skydiver?
She missed Earth.

•

"Brad's a really nice guy, Barbara, and I'm sure you really love him, but how can you bear being married to a quadriplegic?" Cynthia marveled to her gorgeous, blonde, model girlfriend. "He can't even wiggle his little finger. And let's face it: with your face and your body, you could have picked just about any guy on the planet."

"You don't get it, Cyn," replied Barbara. "Who needs fingers? Brad's tongue is eight inches long."

"An eight-inch tongue?" Cynthia gasped.

"And that's not all," continued the blonde smugly. "He's learned to breathe through his ears."

•

Did you hear about the blonde whose husband went ice fishing and brought home one hundred pounds of ice?

She died trying to cook it.

•

How can you tell which motorcycle belongs to the blonde?

It's the one with the training wheels.

•

And which tricycle?

It's the one with the kickstand.

•

Did you hear about the adventurous blonde who got a zebra for a pet?

She named it Spot.

•

The blonde hillbilly had shot her abusive husband point-blank with his turkey gun, and felt a wave of panic come over her as she surveyed the sophisticated-looking jury filing into the courthouse. Positive she'd never beat the murder rap, she managed to get hold of one of the kindlier-looking jurors, and bribe him with a day in the sack to go for a manslaughter verdict.

Sure enough, at the close of the trial the jury declared the hillbilly guilty of manslaughter. Tears of gratitude welling up in her eyes, the young woman had a moment with the juror before being led off to prison. "Thank you, thank you—how'd you do it?"

"It wasn't easy," he admitted. "They all wanted to acquit you."

What did the blonde mermaid sing to the sailors?
  "I can't give you anything but head, baby."

•

What does a man have in his pants that a blonde doesn't want in her face?
  Wrinkles!

•

When the gynecologist confirmed her suspicion that she was pregnant, Celeste got a little scared. "It'll be my first baby," confessed the naive blonde with a blush, "and actually I don't know the first thing about how babies are delivered."

"Don't worry about a thing," reassured the doctor. "It's really not all that different from how the baby got started in the first place."

Startled, Celeste exclaimed, "You mean twice around the park with my legs hanging out of the cab?"

What do you get when you cross a blonde with a pit bull?

Your last blow job.

•

What do you call a blonde anorexic with a yeast infection?

A quarter-pounder with cheese.

•

Mike was touching up the paint in the bathroom one weekend when the brush slipped out of his hand, leaving a stripe across the toilet seat. So Mike painted the whole seat over, and went off to a ball game.

His wife happened to get home early, went upstairs to pee, and found herself firmly stuck to the seat. At six o'clock Mike found her there, furious and embarrassed, but was unable to dislodge her for fear of tearing the skin.

With considerable difficulty Mike managed to get her

into the back seat of the car and then into a wheelchair at the county hospital, where she was wheeled into a room and maneuvered, on her knees, onto an examining table. At this point the resident entered and surveyed the scene. "What do you think, Doc?" broke in the nervous husband.

"Nice, very nice. It's obvious your wife is a natural blonde," he commented, stroking his chin. "But why the cheap frame?"

●

Did you hear about the blonde who had tits on her back?

She was funny to look at, but a whole lot of fun to dance with.

●

What did the blonde say to the long-forgotten friend?

"Undress—I think I know you."

●

What did the lesbian gas station attendant say when the leggy blonde pulled in?

"Mind if I check under your hood?"

•

Blonde Shirley had always wanted to see Australia, so she saved up her money and went off on a two-week tour. And she'd only been there three days when she fell head over heels in love with a kangaroo. So she blithely disregarded the advice of her tour guide and companions, had an aboriginal priest perform a wedding ceremony, and brought her new husband back to her house in the Midwest.

But the new bride found that the course of new love was not without its problems, and in a few months decided to consult a marriage counselor. "Frankly, in your case it's not hard to put my finger on the heart of the problem," said the counselor almost immediately. "Besides the obvious ethnic and cultural differences between you and your . . . ah . . . husband, it's clearly going to be impossible to establish genuine lines of communication with a kangaroo."

"Oh, that's not it at all," broke in the determined blonde. "My husband and I communicate perfectly—except in bed. There it's nothing but hop on, hop off, hop on, hop off. . . ."

•

Judge Wade was considered pretty hard-hearted, but even he was moved by the aging blonde's tale of hardship and woe. Before handing down a sentence he ordered a recess, and was mulling the case over on the way back to his chambers when he ran into a colleague. "Say," he asked, "what would you give a down-and-out, fifty-seven-year-old hooker?"

"Ten bucks, max," replied the other judge.

•

What's the difference between a blonde fox and a blonde pig?

About eight beers.

•

What the biggest advantage to marrying a blonde?

You get to park in the Handicapped Zone.

•

When Alec was informed by his doctor that he had only twelve more hours to live, he rushed home and told his wife, who collapsed in racking sobs. But then the steely blonde pulled herself together, clasped his hands in hers, and promised, "Then I'm going to make tonight the best night of your life, darling." She went out and bought all his favorite delicacies, opened a bottle of fine champagne, served him dinner dressed in his favorite sexy peignoir, and led him up to bed, where she made passionate love to him.

Just as they were about to fall asleep, Alec tapped her on the shoulder. "Honey, could we do it again?"

"Sure, sweetheart," she said sleepily, and obliged.

"Once more, baby?" he asked afterwards. "It's our last night together."

"You bet," she sighed and they made love a third time.

"One last time, darling," he begged a little later, shaking her by the shoulders.

"Well, okay," mumbled the blonde, finally pooped. "But just remember: *you* don't have to get up in the morning."

•

What do you get when you cross a blonde and a computer?

A fucking know-it-all.

What's the difference between a beautiful blonde and a dumpy brunette?

Five or six drinks.

•

The blonde was thrilled to get a jigsaw puzzle for her birthday. She set all sixteen pieces out on a card table and every day when she got home from the office she'd set to work on it. Finally, one day she jumped up from the table and ran to the phone. "Sylvia!" she cried. "Remember the puzzle you gave me? I finished it!"

"Gee, Stacy, that's great," responded her friend after a little hesitation. "But you mean to say it took you three months to put it together?"

"Not bad, eh?" Stacy said proudly. "On the box it says 'Two to five years.'"

•

"I think my new doctor's a crackpot," confessed the blonde to her girlfriend Charlene. "I went to see him about my yeast infection and he told me to drink carrot juice after a hot bath."

"You never know," commented Charlene. "How'd the carrot juice taste?"

"Don't know yet; I've only drunk half the bath so far."

•

Hear about the blonde who didn't dare serve tea to her visitors?

She didn't have a T-shirt!

•

Why did the blonde pee in the middle of the cafeteria?

She saw a sign that read "Wet Floor."

•

Two blondes saved up their money for a week's vacation in Maui. When they reached the hotel, they jumped into their bathing suits and headed for the beach. And no sooner had they waded into the surf than Wanda yelped, "A crab bit one of my toes!"

"Which one?" asked her companion, scurrying back up onto the beach after her.

"How should I know?" Wanda snapped. "All crabs look alike!"

●

What do you call a blonde who can suck a golf ball through fifty feet of garden hose?

Darling.

●

Why does it take brunettes longer to climax?

Who cares?

●

"Now with that entree, either a white wine or a light red would be appropriate," the waiter graciously pointed out. "What may I serve you?"

"Suit yourself," replied the blonde diner cheerfully. "I'm color-blind."

•

The blonde Sweetbriar sophomore spent an extremely daring spring vacation making the rounds of the New York art scene, most of it in the company of a trendy painter named Stuart. And when school was out, she took her parents to Stuart's gala opening.

The walls of the gallery were covered with huge nudes, and Binky's mother lost no time in ascertaining their distinct resemblance to her daughter. Grasping the girl firmly by the elbow and steering her into a quiet corner, she hissed, "Binky, these paintings look just like you. Don't tell me you could have been so tacky as to have posed in the nude."

"Of course not, Mummy," protested the blonde coed, blushing deeply. "Stuart must have painted them from memory!"

•

How can you tell a blonde bitch?
    She thinks she's too good to go fuck herself.

●

A blonde and a brunette both got pregnant at the same time, and had their babies on the same day. And about a year later the blonde came running into her friend's house. "Louise, guess what?" she cried happily. "Little Bobbi said her first word!"

    "Oh yeah?" piped up the brown-haired baby from her playpen in the corner. "What'd she say?"

●

What's the smallest room in the world?
    The Blonde Hall of Virgins.

●

What happened when the blonde bought snow tires for her Firebird?

They melted on the way home.

•

Two aging blonde prostitutes decided they'd had enough of the hard life on the streets, and joined the Salvation Army. Well, Yvonne really took to the new life, but Rhonda had her moments of missing the old, wild days. After a couple of months she admitted to her friend that she just had to go get drunk and laid. And off she went.

It being a Saturday night, Yvonne held her street service in a particularly seamy part of town. And she was just hitting her stride as Rhonda came staggering by with her arm around an equally drunken man. "Friends," preached Yvonne from her Salvation Army soapbox, hitting her stride, "I used to be in the arms of sailors, I used to be in the arms of soldiers, I used to be in the arms of Marines . . . but now I'm in the arms of the Lord."

"Way to go, Yvonne!" yelled Rhonda from the back of the crowd. "Fuck 'em all!"

•

Why don't blonde guys trust blonde girls?

How can you trust someone who bleeds for five days and doesn't die?

·

When Roger met Ruby in a bar one night, he thought the gorgeous blonde was the foxiest creature he'd ever seen, and he remained intrigued even after she'd confessed to having an incredible foot fetish. So he accepted her invitation to come back to her place, and obligingly fucked her with his big toe.

A few days later he woke up with his toe swollen and throbbing. He hobbled over to the doctor, where he was told he had syphilis of the foot. Roger admitted he'd never known such a condition existed. "Is it rare, Doc?"

"Fairly, but I've seen weirder," the doctor told him. "Just this morning a lady came in with athlete's cunt."

·

Hear about the blonde who sent out fifteen hundred perfumed Valentines signed "Guess who?"

She's a divorce lawyer.

What's a blonde's favorite drink?

A Penis Colada!

•

Why couldn't the blonde WAVE get pregnant during the gale at sea?

The seamen kept falling to the floor.

•

The real-estate mogul was delighted by the new, comely blonde receptionist, and proceeded to turn all of his charms upon her. Within a few weeks, however, he grew extremely displeased at her growing tardiness. "Listen, baby," he roared one morning, "we may have gone to bed together a few times, but who said you could start coming in late?"

The secretary replied sweetly, "My lawyer."

•

Why did the promiscuous blonde have a heart like the United States Army?

It was open to any man between the ages of eighteen and thirty-five.

•

The blonde declined to serve on the jury because she was not a believer in capital punishment and didn't want her beliefs to get in the way of a fair trial. "But Madam," said the public defender, who had taken a liking to her, "this is not a murder trial. It is merely a civil lawsuit being brought by a wife against her husband. He gambled away the twelve thousand dollars he'd promised to spend on a sable coat for her birthday."

"Hmmm," mused the blonde. "Okay, I'll serve. I could be wrong about capital punishment."

•

How many blondes does it take to change a light bulb?

None. They like screwing in the dark too.

Did you hear what happened to the blonde who swallowed a razor blade on Monday?

By Thursday she'd given herself a hysterectomy, castrated her husband, circumcised her boyfriend, and given the priest a harelip.

•

"Dr. Bernard completely cured my hemorrhoids," Betty informed the other girls in the secretarial pool. "How'd he do it? First he had me bend over, of course, and then he put one hand on my shoulder and stuck the other up my. . . . Hang on a sec." Betty's face screwed up in concentration, and then she went on. "Yeah, that's it: Dr. Bernard put his right hand on my shoulder and stuck his left up. . . ."

Betty paled. "Wait just a minute!" gasped the blonde. "He had *both* hands on my shoulders!"

•

Why did the blonde cross the road?
  Never mind that, what was she doing out of bed in the first place?

•

What does a blonde do first thing in the morning?
  She goes home.

•

The wealthy blonde matron positively doted on her beloved cat FooFoo. One day she telephoned the vet and insisted he pay a house call. "Her tummy's getting bigger and bigger," she explained. "I'm afraid it's a tumor, Doctor."

It took the vet about two seconds to confirm that little FooFoo was knocked up.

"It can't be!" protested the blonde. "Why, FooFoo never even *sees* another cat. In fact she only leaves the house in her carrying case when I bring her to the Kitty Salon for her shampoo. How could she be pregnant?"

Just then a big tomcat strolled into the room. "What about him?" asked the vet.

"Impossible!" she cried. "That's her brother!"

What was in the blonde spinster's heart-shaped locket?
  A picture of a candle.

•

How does a blonde use a condom twice?
  She turns it inside out and shakes the fuck out of it.

•

The death of a wealthy pillar of the community was the talk of the town for months. After all, his morning coffee had been laced with arsenic by the blonde secretary he'd married two months after the funeral of his wife of thirty years.

Eckhardt, the defense attorney, knew he had his work cut out, and was trying to make his not-very-appealing client appear more sympathetic to the jury. "Tell me, Mrs. Ross, was there any point during the commission of the crime at which you felt pity for your husband?" he asked. Eckhardt was delighted when the voluptuous blonde nodded.

"And when was that?" the lawyer inquired delicately.
"When he asked for a second cup."

●

Why does a blonde have two holes?
So that if she gets drunk, you can carry her home like a six-pack.

●

Why did God invent liquor?
So that brunettes could get laid too.

●

After the plane reached cruising altitude, the captain's voice came over the intercom with the usual information about the speed and altitude, weather conditions and the estimated arrival time. Then, not realizing the microphone was still on, the pilot was heard to say to the co-pilot, "You take over. I'm gonna take a dump and then screw that cute blonde stewardess."

Of course everyone on the plane overheard this indiscreet announcement, and the flight attendant abandoned her beverage cart to dash up to the cockpit and shut off the mike before more damage could be done.

"No need to rush, dearie," said an old woman, grabbing the blonde's elbow as she flew past. "He said he had to go to the bathroom first, remember?"

•

Why was the blonde's second week in Alcoholics Anonymous so much easier than the first one?
By the second week she was drinking again.

•

Why do blondes flock around Army sharpshooters?
They've got a reputation as crack shots.

•

"Daddy, what are those dogs doing?" asked little Tiffany, catching sight of two dogs stuck together in an empty lot during intercourse.

"Uh . . . one dog's hurt and the other one's helping him out, honey," explained her red-faced father hastily.

"What a fuckin' world, huh, Daddy?" commented the little blonde, turning away. "Just when you're down and out, somebody gives it to you up the ass."

●

"This is a little embarrassing, honey," said the hungover husband the morning after a wild party, "but, uh, was it you I made love to out on the balcony last night?"

"Hmmm." The blonde looked up from her Bloody Mary. "About what time?"

●

Why's beauty more important than brains for a blonde?

Because plenty of men are stupid, but not very many are blind.

Would you like to see your favorite tasteless jokes in print—even if they're about redheads or brunettes? If so, send them to:

Blanche Knott
c/o St. Martin's Press
175 Fifth Avenue
New York, N.Y. 10010

I'm sorry, but no compensation or credit can be given. But I *love* hearing from my tasteless readers.